Little BUDDHA

Once upon a time, there was a King Suddhodana. He lived in the kingdom of Kapilvastu along with Queen Mahamaya. After some time the Queen became pregnant. While, going to her maternal home during pregnancy, her health deteriorated. After this she gave birth to a son in the famous garden of Lumbini, away from the kingdom. The King and the Queen named their son Siddhartha.

Unfortunately, the Queen died seven days later after the boy was born. After the death of the Queen, Siddhartha was brought up by his aunt Gautami. Due to being called the son of Gautami, later he was named as Gautam also.

As Siddharth was growing up, an astrologer visited King Suddhodana. He said, "As I can see, in the future your son will either become a king or a beggar. If the prince lives in the palace, he will be a king, or else beggar."

As a result, the King never let his son leave the royal walls. Siddhartha was a bright and cheerful boy. Who was very compassionate and caring.

Siddhartha and his cousin Devadutta were walking in the palace garden one day. Devadutta observed a swan nearby and shot it down on the spot.

Siddhartha was terrified, when he saw the injured bird. He drew the arrow from the swan's body and **applied medicinal herbs to the wound.** His cousin wanted the bird as he shot him, but Siddhartha didn't agree.

As a result, the two boys proceeded to court. In the court, the wise man said that the swan belonged to the person who saved it and not to the one who attempted to take the bird's life.

Soon, Siddhartha matured into a young man. So, King Suddhodana wed him to the beautiful Princess Yashodhara. The King thought, after marriage Siddhartha would never leave his home since he had a wife.

Siddhartha, on the other hand, felt dissatisfied inside the palace walls.

“Let’s take a walk outside the palace!” The Prince urged his servant Channa one day. On their walk, they came upon an elderly man who was hunched over.

While walking, Siddhartha’s eyes fell on an elderly man whose waist was bent. He was walking with a stick. Siddhartha had never seen such an old person before.

He asked Channa, "*Why is this person walking bent over?*"

Channa first looked at the old man and then said softly, "This is an old man. His waist has bent due to increasing age. That is why he walk like this."

Siddhartha asked Channa, "Do all people become like this, when they grow old?"

"Yes, Prince, that is the truth." Channa told

After knowing this, Siddharth's heart trembled. With

lines of worry on his forehead, Siddhartha returned to his palace.

Siddhartha went out of the palace again after a few days.

This time he saw a sick man, *who was wailing in pain.*

Siddhartha asked the servant Channa, "What happened to this man? Why is it moaning?"

Channa said, "*Prince, this man is ill, and is wailing in pain.*"

Seeing this, Siddhartha asked, "Does everyone get sick?"

"Yes prince, the disease does not differentiate between

king or poor, small or big and man or woman. It can happen to anyone."

Hearing Channa's words, the prince became worried.

Both of them had just moved ahead. When they saw some people carrying a dead body.

"Channa what is this?" the prince asked

Channa explained, "Prince, someone has died. These people are going to perform his last rites."

"Why did this person die, Channa?" Siddharth asked

Channa said, "Death is an invariable truth, Prince! This is what everyone in the world has to face."

Just then they saw a man wearing saffron clothes coming. He had shaved his hair. His face was glowing with tenacity and resourcefulness. There was a permanent smile on his lips.

Siddhartha looked at him and asked, "Who is this smiling great man, Channa?"

"This is an ascetic-monk. Which has separated himself from this world. Whatever happens in the world, they remain aloof. This is why he always look happy." Channa replied.

After that the prince decided that he would live a life free from worldly attachments. He decided to set out in search of the truth.

One night, while his wife and son were sleeping, Siddhartha secretly left the palace with his devoted servant, Channa.

They walked together till they reached the Anoma River. The Prince removed his imperial garments there. He handed Channa his clothes and his horse Kanthak to return to the palace. He then shaved his long hair, and walked out.

While wandering, the prince met a famous Acharya, who was engrossed in meditation. Siddhartha learned the virtues of spiritual practice from Acharya.Finally, Siddhartha sat beneath a Peepal tree and attempted to solve the problem independently.

Siddhartha sat down to meditate under a peepal tree. Gradually he attained all four states of meditation. All the past and future started appearing in front of them like a movie. This journey of meditation ended after 14 years. People referred to him as "Gautama Buddha" since he had matured into a knowledgeable man.

Buddha not only cares about humans. But he also cherished all birds and animals, and he treated them with compassion.

Siddhartha's jealous cousin, Devadutta, once dispatched wild elephants to attack Buddha. On the other hand, the *elephants knelt down in front of*

Buddha when they saw him.

Gautam Buddha had five original disciples, who together established the 'Sangha'. All of them followed the teachings and way of life of Buddha.

These five disciples made a special contribution in spreading the messages and teachings of Buddha around the world.

Gautam Buddha advocated that pleasure could be attained by being satisfied with what one had. Also, by treating all beings with kindness.

When he returned to Kapilavastu, he was welcomed by the King, his father, his wife, and his son. Ananda, one of his relatives, became Gautam Buddha's devoted follower and took care of him as he grew older.

Gautam Buddha continued to preach for another 45 years. He was in Kusinara, when a Blacksmith invited him

for dinner. There he ate pudding and became ill. After that he died and attain Mahapari Nirvana.

"A disciplined mind brings happiness."

~Gautam Buddha

An Imprint of Unbound Script

LITTLE BUDDHA

First Edition - Januaury, 2025

ISBN : 978-81-19745-88-3

Publisher
Unbound Script
2/41, Ansari Road, Daryaganj, Delhi - 110002
E-mail : books@unboundscript.com
Website : www.unboundscript.com
Phone No. : 011-35807601

Retold by Kamini Gayakwad

Illustrated by Unbound Script

Printed in India

Price: ₹199/-

An Imprint of Unbound Script

LITTLE BUDDHA

First Edition - Januaury, 2025

ISBN : 978-81-19745-88-3

Publisher
Unbound Script
2/41, Ansari Road, Daryaganj, Delhi - 110002
E-mail : books@unboundscript.com
Website : www.unboundscript.com
Phone No. : 011-35807601

Retold by Kamini Gayakwad

Illustrated by Unbound Script

Printed in India

Price: ₹199/-